Cicada Song

poems by

Ryan Norman

Finishing Line Press
Georgetown, Kentucky

Cicada Song

ACKNOWLEDGMENTS

Labyrinth—*Fully Lit Magazine*
Stars Fall—*Black Bough Poetry Freedom*/Rapture (print)
Unblinking—*Broken Spine Artist Collective* Issue 2 (print)
Delicate—*All Guts No Glory*
Summer Snow—*BRAG* Writers Issue 1 (print)
Crashing—*Lucky Pierre Literary Magazine*
Cleansed—*Fully Lit Magazine*
Cicada Song—*3 Moon Magazine*—Metamorphosis
Waterlogged—*Icefloe Press*—Mother/Service/Voice
Meditation in Water – *Neologism Poetry Journal* – August 2020
Ash Flames to Dust—*Black Bough Poetry*—Christmas/Winter Edition (print)
Apple Passage—*Black Bough Poetry*—Deep Time Vol. 2 (print)
Petrichor—*Floodlight Editions*
Lake Nights—*Elephants Never*
Preen—*3 Moon Magazine* —Metamorphosis
Breaking Ground—*Floodlight Editions*
The Moon is my Mother—*All Guts No Glory*
New Year—*3 Moon Magazine*—Metamorphosis
This Will Change Your Life—*Brave Voices Magazine*

Publisher: Leah Huete de Maines
Editor: Christen Kincaid
Cover Art: Dev Murphy
Author Photo: Ryan Norman
Cover Design: Elizabeth Maines McCleavy

Order online: www.finishinglinepress.com
also available on amazon.com

Author inquiries and mail orders:
Finishing Line Press
PO Box 1626
Georgetown, Kentucky 40324
USA

Table of Contents

" ... everything in life is writable about if you have the outgoing guts to do it, and the imagination to improvise."

Sylvia Plath

Labyrinth

Waves crashed against his labyrinth, blowing back
his hair as he stared into the angry sea,
a welcome gray, white capped,
unable to corrode his hand placed stone,
mortared by memories cemented in time.

The sea's wet breath whispered seductive secrets
of escape, but to where?
A drum beat in the distance, steadying his racing heart.
A ship sailed the horizon,
cheapening his plan of counting crests,

breaking to sea-debris against his fortification.
The albatross circled above. He slinked
into the shadows afraid
of what was to come.
Horns trumpeted; cymbals crashed.

Sounds of celebration drew him
from his quarters:
curiosity killed the discrete.
Spied by dark eyes, penetrating his fortress,
reaching out a hand, he backed against

the balustrade and leapt,
albatross-free
falling.
His labyrinth faded in the
plummet.

One drop in the ocean.
Tossed and tumbled.
Spat out like sea trash,
stung by a sandpaper tongue,
bottled, no postage, return to sender;

into the arms of a stranger.
You look freshly plucked, my goosefleshed, fledgling Icarus.
His limp body tossed over a shoulder, taken back inside,
as he looked back at the sea as it
waved.

Rust

Careening around hairpin turns,
trestles quaking, metal on metal,
as his car tires kiss guardrails

guarding a 50-foot cliff,
spitting loose stone over the edge
listening for the crack

of stone splitting stone,
he held the steering wheel
pale-gripped. Pressing on,

faster and faster,
more reckless than anyone would expect of him,
his heart beat a heavy bass

until his whole body trembled,
his breath becoming
chesty and quick.

How quickly this turned from a normal,
long drive on serpentine roads,
winding through a mountain town, to a fight

to catch breath, numb fingered, tear filled eyes.
His foot, leaden, raced to an abandoned parking lot,
lit by a fluorescent moonbeam,

where he parked to watch himself cry
in a fingerprinted rearview
gathering the strength to look down,

pull back the bandage, brown and rust,
to reveal a jagged line
as straight as the roads he traveled.

Stars Fall

I

Moonlight ripples, unabashed, down your naked form;
intoxicated confidence bared on slick stone, water roars
and splashes wet stars—skin glows constellations.

II

Pressing my nakedness into his,
we are two crescents waxing full.

III

Light leaks morning across blank flesh,
flashing spotted memories, connecting dots—
its golden finger traces your landscape,
warming skin still chilled from
a late night swim.

Unblinking

The hood was still warm
from the drive to the upper orchard.
The truck growled over the terrain.

Tonight, I was your ornament,
reclined against the glass, hanging on your arm.
The night sky, dappled with stars,

swirled as I toasted my cider
to the Queen of the Night:
crescent-crowned,

the only still thing,
unblinking,
unphased by her satellite swing,

silvered your eyes and slivered mine,
as I beamed, wondering if I
would sleep for a spell,

so you could look at me
forever like that.

Delicate

His hands held a bird,
nesting in palms
creased with lines heavy

in work. Its wet eyes blinked
black glass,
damp with a mournful song.

Its feathers, greased for a day
of flight stopped short
by the broadside of a barn;

they swapped oils, foreigners
exchanging gifts at a chance meeting,
each needing the other

without knowing.
A mended wing
full of breadth,

its bones complex and hollowed
to breathe in flight. His fingers,
blood and marrow, delicate

despite their strength,
raised a bird, red chest beating,
to fly again.

Paint

Shattered flames cut glass, splinter sharp,
leaving behind blade shards

to the cutting sound of electric guitars
dueling pianos trapped in a speaker

breaking decibel codes across a summer town,
with one eye closed to the

picket-fenced home
housing a squeaky-clean teenager,

reputation intact, popped polo collar,
pressed against peeling paint,

one wall of a box, stuck inside perfection
biting leather, draining insecurities,

dodging dangerous questions with painted smiles.
Desperate for escape, he blasts music

shouting revolutions, to cuffed ears
screaming: *we can't hear your truth.*

Tightening blindfolds
'til they see stars instead of scars.

Summer Snow

My sun-blushed cheeks reach apple heights
when I see you cresting the driveway;

footfalls crunching on summer snow. And the heavy sweat
and streaks of dirt swiped across your brow

are now rising at the sight of me—sitting here
on the tailgate of your pick-up truck.

I see you exaggerate your saunter, hiding a dandelion
behind one hand like a birthday candle

that you hold to my lips and say:
                    One thousand wishes for one breath ...

and the seeds float off to propagate fields
or wherever the wind takes them, like snowflakes.

Feeling your lips press mine, I close my eyes to capture
this moment

and ask: *wanna fuck?*

Crashing

It was a foot race down the yellowing path, sunburnt grass, a downtrodden history marked the center lane between overgrown forsythia, butter-melt in the heat to its ravaged leaves, aphid love bites. We howled past the weather-worn shed, white-washed flakes splintered to the weed-brimmed window box—a shoe flew by and then another, until anyone could find us by following the clothing trail, down to the creek bed where we dove into the barely known of one another, drinking with our eyes an unquenchable thirst in side glances. We steamed, lava hot, in the icy water. I watched you float as a waterfall crashed harder than I did for you.

Cleansed

We showered under the Buck moon,
one hot summer night, mid-July.
Your celestial body refracted the light—

launching water flecked stars into the inky night,
replacing constellations as they faded to black.
Time had no meaning.

Just us.
The summer.
A pin-pricked sky.

Sandalwood and apples permeated the orchard air.
Crickets chirped a scattered song in the tall grass:
a summer song in our amphitheater,

echoing in a domed atmosphere, closing in.
Stars burst, pyrotechnic, welting skin
unable to be soothed by the breeze

crescendoing into gusts. The sky opened,
doubly cleansed, in a ritual moon bath.
We walked together, one step, two.

Synchronized. Fingers entwined,
pressed between the sheets, stark white.
With wet eyes, a whisper: *I don't love you.*

Moments before, we were ready to jump
into a chariot and light the sky.
How easily a flame can extinguish.

Run Me Like A River

I climb the dirt bank to the river's shore, lapping like a thirsty predator, head bowed deeply, smoothing broken beer glass to river stone, with my heart pulsing in hand. Will you solve a riddled body one last time if I submerge my soul, on fire, or snuff me out like a flickering flame playing with chemistry? I'm drawn to the power of your whispering waves that grow into a scream like a locomotive's heavy truths: he's betrayed me. I skip my once muscle-bound heart like a flat stone across your tumultuous surface counting one, two, sunk. My answer, stone heavy, passed over by the bottom feeders.

Cicada Song

Slumbering in underground cradles,
dirt-nymphs, dreaming of Athenian
ancestors' gilded bodies pinning
ancient tendrilled locks—

birthed from the soil, autochthonous
to apple carcass sediment
eager to shed our youthful shells,
we dried in the sun beside

your glistening likeness stamped on
silver thrown at your feet.

My new skin hardening over time
watching sunsets alone
in the boughs we claimed
together, with your song

choose me, choose me
to watch you fly off
as I lay among the misted
orchard with wet wings

and receive a message in the wind:
you're singing for someone new.

Waterlogged

I watched you in the dark and your dark
became my dark.

To come home and find you
with your back against the cushions, curled

against the world, heavy
curtains blocking out all that light.

I'd look at your sadness
and feel

for a smile, my fingers
fumbling

over crevasses filled with tears. Their
waterlogged prints unrecognizable

from searching so long. I used
to wish that I could hug you

the way the couch did and feel
your warmth.

But I went to my room,
closed the curtains,

and let the darkness hug me
instead.

Meditation in Water

Tonight, I meditated under a waning moon,
     my intentions modest,
      a quiet connection
driven through bared soles, resting
in puddles on a dark   balcony.

Did I feel the draw of the dark?
Was Selene pulling   my water as I sat
spellbound, less wooden, more liquid,
tidal?

Sloshing between her world and mine,
despite the grounding,
      tethered by gravity, lassoed by stars
      —rising. Above

what stands rooted: forests.
Into
what moves in me: rivers.
But
in exhalation, it disappeared,

      and I sat with
      wet feet on a

damp porch
as reality buzzed by.

This Will Change Your Life

This energy crosses a synapse
and electrifies movement across time,
space. I hear your laughter and it
peels layers, breaks barriers as we forget
how delicate life can be;

we sit so close, eyes closed, and
transfer breath
across gaps in memories to bring them
back to life. Spark a relic buried deep
in the dusty caverns

on exhale. Inhale its truth. Light a
purpose with a singular wink.
Vibrant beyond auras out-glowing
auras. Still in stillness. 'This will change
your life'. Even when synapses don't fire,
you do.

Ash Flames to Dust

Buried to my knees, ice-soled,
I call for Brighid to light
the dark, to shoulder my burden:

In the distance,
the Ash tree
flames to dust.

Apple Passage

I

A woman shrouded in mist
draws me to the sea extending
a fruit-bearing branch, her song

a promise to the otherworld.
I pluck my apple, passage
to a ghost ship. Sea-brined air

takes bites at its flesh
leaving only seeds
inside my quaking palm—

the silver-cloud parts
on shore unveiling
a torch-lit cavern
under an apple tree.

II

The old tree above
takes deep breaths

inflating the cavern's
underland.

Heavy mists suffocate
the torch once illuminating

umbilical roots,
feeding the hungry maw

that swallowed souls
searching for peace
in the afterlife.

Baby Breath

I came into this world headfirst, blue-faced, the voice choked out of me by the one thing giving me life. I've spoken of umbilical roots as a metaphor of a tree feeding souls into a dark cave as they transitioned into another life, but I've never spoken of my umbilical roots. The roots that stole my newborn voice. My baby breath. She should have known the care I would need—blue to this world with an umbilical noose. How I would cry, and cry, twisted in emotions with no voice. Forever entangled, between fingers, purse strings, her voice, his voice.

I cried until my breath stopped, blue again, blue always. Tangled in the wires, crossing, sparking. I stood by her side, by his side; but I always hung upside down in my own life and learned to see things from the bottom. Around each corner, the torment of lassoed rope. The shadow of a noose. A reminder of my roots. No matter the successes, the connections, truth always leaked in my lungs. Until I stayed with him on a lake and it called me in.

So, I called her, the lasso had its hold. And I walked through sprinklers, wetting me so the slip was easy. How I would struggle to say *help me* as I waded back into the water, trying to breathe fluid once again, under the moon; her voice calling from the shore one thousand miles away, our lines entangled, as I sank into the glimmering darkness.

Petrichor

Remember the time we
walked on wet leaves?
You said the stench of their decay

reminded you of me. I like to think
that it's the smell of fresh rainfall
and not   dead leaves.

That maybe it's the
                bouquet of an earthy breath.
Maybe a memory.

Like the time we slept in a tent
and it   poured,
so we held each other for warmth.

There was a smell then
that is hard to articulate.
Maybe you really meant dead leaves.

Black Skies

I should have said no but I didn't.
What's wrong with a beer in a hipster bar
in the dead of winter with someone who
ate your heart and told you to

buck up, dry your tears,
offered you his bloodstained shirt
covered in your plans of forever,
a home, children,

because you should have seen it coming?
You're embarrassing yourself.
Why not open up to him?
Tell him you've been in therapy for months.

Tell him grad school isn't looking good. Not since he left.
He says you're blaming him. But he's the one
dating the adulterer. That's why he called you.
To be with someone normal. And here you are,

yet again, making things weird. He tells you
he's been working out. Grabs your hand
and puts it on his flexed bicep.
Tells you that you like it to your flushed face.

There are people all around. He tips the bartender
and takes you back to his car. Climbs on you
like you're teenagers without private homes.
Rips your favorite wool coat. Buttons take too long.

You go back to his home on the orchard,
to the renovated pigsty. The sky is black.
The snow crunches underfoot. You push him
against the wall, pressing your body onto his.

The yellow flag with the black coiled snake
falls to the ground. You tread on it.
His voice gets angry, but his body tells a different story.

Lake Nights

Moonlight laps the shoreline as
tiny-surfed feet dance on the pebbles
in the stillness of night.
Soft crashes of water on stone orchestrate
a ceremonious march toward sirens'
soft sonnets—vows of forever
together in the depths of the shallow
glittered lake.

His steps sink in the man-sown sand
covering the beach of dirt and stone his
heel toe, heel toe sliding
one after the other—
Soles pound to the sound of the tree frogs
behind him progressing in dream-like
strides to the hush, hush of the little
crashing waves.

Cold-footed, his toes dig deep against
the pull of a mind poisoned by
years of his voice echoing
in a void reverberating answers of
years past propelling him
toe first, testing the waters
warmed by moon beams to
take the plunge.

Weighted jeans heavy with vacillations of 'wait,
no, go' fill cotton-twilled fabric with the
lake's tiny feet that once danced on the shore
now crawl up his chest soaked
in 'what if' and 'I don't'.
Sound becomes silence in sobs
of tears glistening in the moonlight
beaming truths.

Flooding the void
deafened the voice.

Preen

Ten years I was a caged bird
barred by a pill construct:
Pop, swig, smile.

In therapy I'd preen
feathers out of place:
Pop, swig, smile.

They said it would end
with every new pill:
Pop, swig, smile.

The day finally came;
A new diagnosis—
'Forever,' slithered in my ear.
Preen, little bird. Smile.

Solace

Fingers splay stone-cold solace
to shelter-in-place in the hands
of ancient strangers—

ghosts in silhouette—
welcome with rusted intentions
a world incubating disease

into a cold cave's
warm embrace.

Breaking Ground

Have you ever stood next to a tree, boxed
in with cement, and cried for its strength?
Red eyes on the rippled sidewalk,
where the roots reach

for nourishment;
to thrive beyond their stunted
forever.
Breaking ground, busting pipes.

Wreaking havoc on the structure
that confines it,
as it lives and changes
despite its small square.

Have you ever touched its scars?
The ones left by
bicycle chains. Lovers.
And yet it drops its leaves,

staining the cement watercolors
every year. Holding the weight
of winter, bracing the cold.
Budding in protest, it grows.

The Moon Is my Mother

I'm water all the time, since I left you
on the shore to shout against the tiny
wake of the lake's wet feet. I pushed
    against the weight

of water tugging at my shirt
and stared into the cratered face
    of the moon, more battered

than me. She pulled my tides,
revealed hidden parts of me.
Her crescent crown illuminated my
downfall.

Her voice called into my body,
shivered me. Shoulder deep,
she grasped my arms and pulled
me back to shore, where I laid,
all water—to confirm the moon
is my mother now.

New Year

Blue flames lick at
my splintered foundations,
a nest of a home
for an over-preened pigeon,

curr, curring at reptilian
toes tracking ash from
one calendar to the next—
A phoenix lives next door.

Flying into a new year,
a bird's eye view of
what ought to be
and what ought not.

Ryan Norman (he/him) is the author of the pop culture poetry chapbook "I Always Wanted to be a Bond Girl" (The Daily Drunk Press). He also currently serves as contributing creative nonfiction editor for *Barren Magazine*. A native New Yorker, Ryan is influenced by the mountains and lakes. He studied psychology in New York City, but ultimately returned to his roots in the Catskills. Recent work appears in *Black Bough Poetry, Maudlin House, From Whispers to Roars, Hobart Pulp, HAD,* and *X-R-A-Y Literary Magazine.*

When not writing you can find Ryan in a mountain or along a river. You can find a sampling of his writing on ryanmgnorman. com or follow him on Twitter @ryanmgnorman to keep up with his thoughts.